THROUGH
THE
EASTERN GATE

AN ANTHOLOGY OF CHRISTIAN POETRY

by

SUE WILDING

HORSESHOE PUBLICATIONS
KINGSLEY, WARRINGTON
CHESHIRE

ISBN 1 899310 02 9

First published 1995 by
HORSESHOE PUBLICATIONS
Box 37, Kingsley, Warrington,
Cheshire WA6 8DR

Book cover designed by Cheshire Artist
TRACY WALKDEN

Printed and bound in Great Britain by
ANTONY ROWE LTD
Chippenham, Wiltshire

JANUARY

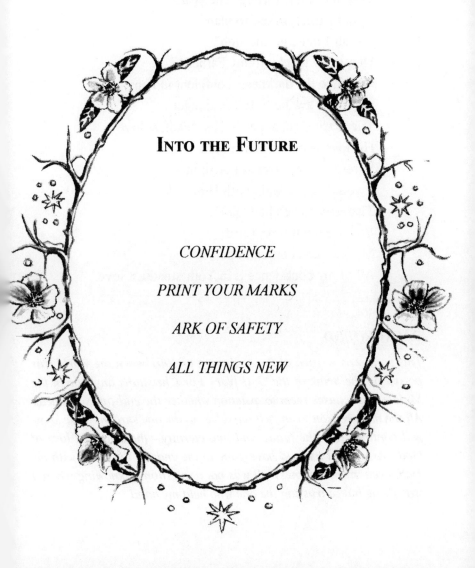

INTO THE FUTURE

CONFIDENCE

PRINT YOUR MARKS

ARK OF SAFETY

ALL THINGS NEW

CONFIDENCE

If I could look behind the curtain
And see for certain what the future holds
Could I prepare for each tomorrow
For joy or sorrow, would it give me hope?
Would knowing banish all my fear
Take me safely through the year
Could I trust myself to plan
For all I must go through?
I'll put my hand into my Father's
And face the darkness, confident in Him
Though I awake to toil or danger
There are no changes in His steadfast love
His love is better than a light
Surer than my strength or sight
I would rather walk with Him
Than tread each path alone
You are my future, Lord
My sure and certain hope
All of my confidence is in Your steadfast love.

BACKGROUND

This song was written at the beginning of 1991 when the world was poised on the brink of the Gulf War. For Christians any war in the Middle East causes them to question whether the end-times are near. All the more reason to entrust ourselves to the one sure thing we know will continue into the future and into eternity - the steadfast love of God. As a child I would have gone to the ends of the earth with my Dad, even in the darkness. It was not a question of knowing where I was going but of trusting the one who held my hand.

PRINT YOUR MARKS

You know my story well
The pages in Your book lie open still
You know when life began
And how to write all things into Your plan
And in Your heart - more plans and dreams
You're longing to fulfil
waiting only till I let You
Shape them as You will
If I should fall and spoil Your plot
By sin or pride
If I should blot Your pages with disgrace
I know that You'll search
For ways to still redeem and restore
Out of Your love
Out of Your skill
Out of Your grace
Oh, Jesus, Saviour, print Your marks
Of truth upon my heart
And from my life let others read
Your patience and Your art.

BACKGROUND

In this song Jesus is seen as the Author of the book of our lives. He has a masterplan in mind as he writes but, if we spoil it by our waywardness, all is not lost. In His skill He can turn our failures and mistakes into vital parts of the story. Through Jesus all things are redeemable. As others watch the story of our lives unfold they too will be amazed at the skill and grace of God.

JESUS, MY ARK OF SAFETY

In my great love I built a boat
An ark to keep you from the grave
I named it "Jesus" and it floats
Above the high and stormy waves

Salvation lies within its walls
Your soul has found a resting place
Secure in Me your anchor will hold
At journey's end a rainbow waits

And though at times you feel confined
Your faith and patience fully stretched
Plans for your future fill My mind
My purposes I'll not forget

Be still and know that I am God
Exalted high My name shall be
Above the Kingdoms of this world
And you, My child, will be with Me

BACKGROUND

Reading the story of Noah and the ark prompted the writing of this song. The ark is such a graphic symbol of the salvation which is found in Jesus. Once we are "in Him" the destructive flood waters of judgement cannot touch us. Conditions in the ark during the long weeks of the flood must have been quite stressful at times. God, however, had Noah's times in His hand. The future held joy and promise as symbolised by the rainbow. For us, as Christians, the ultimate future is full of glorious hope despite times when the present holds only gloom and doom. We need to keep the example of Noah before us.

ALL THINGS NEW

A new heart, I have given you a new heart
A heart that is tender and warm
Replacing your stony indifference
Your coldness toward me
A heart for My home

A new mind, I have given you a new mind
A mind that is open and pure
Believing and knowing My power
Receiving My word now
Obeying My law

A new way, I have made for you a new way
A way to My Father above
Approaching right into His presence
The bridge is My body
The highway of love

New wine, I have poured for you the new wine
The wine of My Spirit in you
Receive Him with praise and rejoicing
He'll fill you with gladness
He'll make all things new

BACKGROUND

At the beginning of a new year we often make resolutions hoping that, by our will power, we can make changes in our lives. This can only be successful to a certain extent. God is the only one who can make radical changes in us by the Holy Spirit. The life which is open to Him will be constantly renewed and energised. As Revelation chapter 21 verse 5 says, 'He does indeed make all things new'.

FEBRUARY

REFRESHMENT

COME UNTO ME

LIKE A DEER

PSALM 63

SOMETIMES MY SOUL IS WEARY

COME UNTO ME

Come unto Me all you heavy-laden
You who are weary and longing for rest
Come and learn of Me for My yoke is easy
I'm humble and gentle, My way is best.

Come unto Me all you hungry and thirsty
I am the Bread of life. My flesh was given for you
And from my open heart flows a fountain of water
A stream of refreshing, a source ever new.

Come unto me all you poor and needy
Come and discover all the riches in Me
My heart is full of love and My arms are laden
With gifts from my storehouse of treasures for you.

BACKGROUND

This song is based on the open invitation of the Lord Jesus at the end of Matthew Chapter 11. How His hearers must have eagerly soaked up those gentle, soothing words. No-one, except perhaps the self-sufficient, is excluded from this gospel invitation nor from the other calls to feed and drink from Jesus. He longs to give everyone rest and refreshment just like the good shepherd He is. The undeniable proof of His love is that He gave His flesh for us at Calvary.

LIKE A DEER

Like a deer in the forest
Being chased by the hunters
Exhausted from running
And longing for rest
I am thirsty for You, Lord
And Your streams of cool water
Flowing down from Your mountains
To keep me refreshed
Come, let me taste You
Sweet fountain of blessing
Let me drink from Your mercy
In your love let me rest
Let me wait as You take now
All the weariness from me
In Your presence, Lord Jesus,
My soul is refreshed.

BACKGROUND

This song is based on psalm 42 where the writer describes his soul as a thirsty deer. This is a very graphic image of times in our lives when the only satisfaction we can find is in the stream of life which is in Jesus. The deer which plunges into water receives relief in many ways. He is immediately safe from his predators which will not pursue him into this foreign element. His overheated system is restored to normality. The slaking of his thirst refreshes and revitalizes his life. All traces of any tracks are removed as he wades into the stream. In similar ways the exhausted Christian receives cleansing, forgiveness and the removal of guilt as he bathes in the cool waters of the presence of Jesus.

PSALM 63

Earnestly seeking You, Lord, I thirst
In a dry, weary land for drink and rest
I long for You.

Let me see, once again, visions of You
In your love, in Your power, my zeal renew
To worship You.

I would give up my life, in exchange
For the riches of your love, to know Your embrace
I cherish You.

Staying close by Your side, I will sing
Of Your grace and Your care overshadowing
I rest in You.

BACKGROUND

This psalm was written when David was in the desert of Judah, fleeing from Saul. Physically and spiritually he was parched, longing for rest and for the quenching of his thirst. The spiritual, however, becomes paramount and David determines to keep a song of praise on his lips as he remembers his God. He has confidence to believe that God will bring him back to the sanctuary. In the meantime, even if he were to face death in the desert, he is sure of one thing - God's unfailing love for him.

SOMETIMES MY SOUL IS WEARY

Sometimes my soul is weary
Reluctant to give praise
Sometimes I feel discouraged
Longing only for escape
But then your Spirit kindles
A deep fire within
And warms my heart to Jesus
Stirring worship just for Him
I love You, Jesus
I cannot but sing
Declaring Your praises
My Saviour, My King
And though I can't measure
In words of a song
How great is Your mercy
How deep or how strong
Yet I will give glory
For all that I know
For You are the rock of refuge
To which I can always go.

BACKGROUND

Even the psalmist admitted that there were times in his life when he wished he had the wings of a dove to escape from his circumstances. Sometimes the last thing we want to do is praise God. However, the Holy Spirit is able to overcome our weariness and reluctance. He is always ready to give glory to Jesus and will cause us to sing to Him too. As we consider the immeasurable love of God our spirits will be caught up in worship time and time again.

MARCH

WINGS

PSALM 91

SPREAD YOUR WINGS

THE DOVE

FREEDOM

PSALM 91

The Lord is my refuge
And under His wings
I dwell in the safety
His faithfulness brings
No terror of darkness
No arrow of fear
No evil can taunt me
Or reach me in here
A thousand may fall beside me
Ten thousand at my right hand
His angels will keep me
Wherever I tread
No harm shall befall me
No ill will I dread

BACKGROUND

The main image in this song is of the Lord as a huge, protective bird who covers those who come to Him for shelter. The wings of the Lord form an impregnable shield against nightmarish fears which attack the believer. All who trust in God will find He always places Himself between the believer and disaster. The cross is the best example of this.

SPREAD YOUR WINGS

Father, like the eagle, stir Your nest
Teach Your little ones to fly
When we fall spread out Your wings beneath us Lord
Bear us ever upwards
Carry us until we learn Your ways
That we might soar up to the heavens
That we might see the distant view
That we might dwell in higher places
Swift and strong just like You

Spirit, like the dove, come close to us
Dwell within our house, we pray
Flutter through each room and fill it with Your peace
Come to us and heal us
Comfort us and ever with us stay
That You might bless us with Your music
That we might learn Your gentle ways
That Your influence might make us
Holy like You

Jesus, Lord, You long to gather us
Like a hen beneath Your wing
There protect us from the evil one
Let us feel Your warmth, Lord
Shelter us from every harmful thing
That we might know how much You love us
That we might feel Your beating heart
That in safety we might grow up
To be just like You

BACKGROUND

In this song we see the different ministries of the God-head described as three birds. God the Father is like the majestic parent eagle who longs for us to learn how to soar in heavenly places. The Holy Spirit is like the gentle dove bringing healing and peace into our lives. The Lord Jesus, in His protective care for us, is like the mother hen which shelters its little ones under her wing. In all these ways we are to grow up to be like our Lord.

THE DOVE

Open the eyes of your soul and behold
My Spirit, He hovers above
Waiting to settle in welcoming hearts
To deliver My message of peace to you
For My Spirit, He comes like a dove

Gently and sweetly He'll sing to your soul
Or He'll heal with the touch of His wing
Or He'll show you My Jesus as never before
Revealing His beauty again to you
For I sent Him to glorify Him

BACKGROUND

The presence of the Holy Spirit has often been depicted by the image of a dove. He was the Spirit brooding over the waters before creation. He also descended upon Jesus in bodily form like a dove at His baptism. When the Spirit of God is present at a meeting we are often conscious of Him hovering like a bird, wanting to minister to us. He is gentle and peaceable, never forcing His way in. Sometimes He may manifest himself through healing. Other times He may bring us into a fuller revelation of the beauty of Jesus. Always He works in harmony with the other persons of the Godhead.

FREEDOM

My freedom is for you
I died to take your bonds away
I long to break the ties
And shatter every bond today
Come away, Oh My love
Take My wings and fly
Soar with Me, like a dove
Through the pathless sky
I liberate you now
Escape free from your prison hold
Be loosed from all your fears
Prepare yourself for flight
Be bold.

BACKGROUND

Although Paul often described himself as a bond-slave of Jesus he also makes many references to spiritual freedom. Jesus said.. "if the Son sets you free, you will be free indeed". (John 8 verse 36). The liberty he was talking about was being able to shake off the shackles of sinfulness and fear. Jesus is the great emancipator. He invites us to escape from our bondages and soar in the Spirit as He intended us to. We are not obliged to continue in restricted patterns of life. He died to release us.

EASTER SECTION

NOW MY SOUL IS OVERWHELMED

DESPISED AND REJECTED

RISEN LORD

PETER'S SONG

NOW MY SOUL IS OVERWHELMED

Now My soul is overwhelmed with sorrow
Powers of darkness gather for the morrow
Father, shall I pray that You take this cup away?
Yet, how else shall I your purposes fulfil?
Father, I surrender to Your will

Many terrors threaten and surround Me
Beasts of prey encircle to devour Me
Night replaces day as You turn Your face away
I cry out to You and offer up My breath
I have poured My soul out unto death

In My tomb I have buried
All man's darkest sins
Death and hell have a hold on him no more
By My cross I have opened heaven's door
He will live as he's never lived before

Brightly dawns My day of resurrection
You have kept My Body from corruption
From My death springs peace
Joy and healing and release
I have undergone Your fire and Your knife
That those we love might share our endless life

BACKGROUND

This song seeks to gain insight into the physical, mental and spiritual agonies which Jesus went through in Gethsemane and at Calvary. These are depths which we can never really plumb except through the Holy Spirit. Yet the depths turn to heights of joy and release as the song ends considering the blessings which have resulted from the cross.

DESPISED AND REJECTED

He was despised and rejected
A man acquainted with sorrow
He had no beauty or glory
That we should desire Him
Too ashamed to receive Him
We turned our faces away

Surely He carried all our sin and sorrow
His death brought us peace
And by His stripes we are healed

He was oppressed and afflicted
And led away to the slaughter
Like a lamb who is dumb
Or a sheep before her shearers
Silently He was taken
Without a cry of resistance

He was cut off from the living
Stricken for our transgression
Crucified with the wicked
And the rich gave His grave
Though we considered Him smitten
It was the Lord's will to crush Him

When His travail is ended
Once again He will flourish
For His suffering will bring forth
Many children of God
Sons and daughters to give Him
The praise He richly deserves

BACKGROUND

The beautiful prophetic passage in Isaiah 53 is the basis for this song. From this same scripture Philip preached Jesus to the Ethiopian eunuch. (See Acts 8 verse 35). Although much of the song concentrates on the suffering of Christ it ends with resurrection and praise. The one whose great suffering bought us so much deserves the best we can give Him.

RISEN LORD

Come and see the place where Jesus lay
His tomb is empty
Come and greet the risen Lord
Come and celebrate
This glorious day of resurrection
Come and greet the risen Lord
Gone is death and darkness
Fear and sorrow
Dawns a bright new morrow
News will be preached in every nation
News of forgiveness and salvation
Leave all doubt behind
Make up your mind
That you will trust Him
Come and greet the risen Lord
On the cross He took
Your sin and sorrow
All of your tomorrows
He'll fill with hope and expectation
Come to Him now
Your God is waiting
Leave all doubt behind
Make up your mind
That you will trust Him
Come and greet the risen Lord

BACKGROUND

*The empty tomb is one of the central truths of the Christian faith. In 1
Corinthians chapter 15 Paul tells us that if Christ is not risen then our
faith is in vain. This song is an invitation to reach out to the risen Lord
in faith and love. We need to greet him as warmly as He greeted the
disciples after the resurrection. Easter is a time for rejoicing, for giving
up doubt and for believing in all our tomorrows. Living in the reality
of His presence gives us hope for the future.*

PETER'S SONG

You ask me if I love You
I say, "Lord, You know all things
You know my limitations
My failures and my sins"
But how can I not love You
When I look into Your face
So full of expectation
My answer, Lord, is "Yes"
While your Spirit lends me breath
I will praise You for your death
Though I denied You
I now own You Lord
All my questions and my plans
I submit into Your hands
For Your love has won
The right to rule my life
Your love has forced an answer
And looked into my eyes
Your love has lifted up my head
And taught me not to lie

BACKGROUND

This song is based on the searching question Jesus asked of Peter after the resurrection. Repeatedly Jesus asks "Do you love Me?" (John chapter 21 verses 15 - 22). The repetition is reminiscent of the three times Peter denied Jesus. It must have been a painful reminder but the purpose of this encounter was not to condemn. It was to reinstate and recommission the repentant disciple. Peter's affirmation was as much for himself as it was for Jesus. However it must always bless the heart of the Lord when our answer to this question is "Yes".

APRIL

COMFORT

ISAIAH 61

HE'S MY BROTHER

BEAUTY FOR ASHES

WHENEVER

ISAIAH 61

Sovereign Lord, Your Spirit rests
On me, Your chosen
The One that You have sent
Sent to proclaim
Good news to the poor
The favour of the Lord
And You have placed
Into My hands
Power to deliver
Power to break all bonds
To give back sight
To eyes that once were blind
To heal the sick and lame
And I will bind up
All the broken hearts
I will comfort all who mourn
Yes, I will bring relief
To those who grieve
I will give to them
A crown of beauty

BACKGROUND

In Luke chapter 4 verses 18 - 20 we read how Jesus quoted this old testament passage in the synagogue at Nazareth and claimed that its fulfilment was in Him. What a dramatic moment that must have been when all eyes were fixed on Him. It is wonderful to trace the fulfilment of this prophecy in the works of Jesus and his followers. An even more amazing thought is that the Spirit rests on us for the same purpose in this day and age. We are meant to be instruments of physical and emotional healing as we go forth proclaiming the good news of Jesus to the poor.

HE'S MY BROTHER

The way ahead is sometimes so hard to see
The road seems too rough and I'm no pioneer
But I'm not the first for someone has gone before
His name is Jesus
He's my brother

And when I think there's no-one to understand
No-one who can share the trials and the pain
I know I'm not alone. There's someone to comfort me
His name is Jesus
He's my brother

When friends grow cold and no-one will stand by me
Surrounded by foes I fear all help is gone
No more am I a stranger
But part of His family
God is my father
Jesus is my brother

BACKGROUND

In the Christian family we can enjoy the benefits of knowing God as our Father and Jesus as our older brother. Being the eldest of three children I never had an older brother but sometimes felt I would like to have done. In every sense Jesus is the big brother who has been through everything we are likely to experience. He can therefore advise, comfort and encourage us on our journey. Best of all He goes with us.

BEAUTY FOR ASHES

I will provide beauty for ashes
The oil of joy instead of grief
Your heaviness will turn to singing
For I will comfort all who mourn

And all the years you thought were wasted
Their ravages beyond repair
I will repay you for all losses
I will redeem, I will restore

Oh restless one, forever seeking
A love to fully satisfy
I've chosen you, I will betroth you
For evermore to be My bride

And when in cries of desolation
Your orphan-spirit to Me calls
I will enfold you in My presence
That is My name, Emmanuel

BACKGROUND

When all we seem to be left with are the ashes of our lives God promises relief and comfort. Indeed there seem to be many indications in the scriptures that God has a special place in his heart for those who mourn. Maybe this is because Jesus himself was called a "man of sorrows, acquainted with grief". (Isaiah 53). He is the redeemer who compensates us for the sense of loss we feel. For those of us who are lonely or unloved He is both the eternal Father and the faithful Bridegroom.

WHENEVER

When you're weary
When the heat is on
When there's no place to hide
And the sun is beating down
I'll cover you, I'll be your rock
My shadow will provide
Shelter from storm and wind and desert
Come to My shade

When you're thirsty
When your life is dry
When you're too weak to walk
I will come to you, I'll lift your head
And cause you to drink
Until your soul revives
From My rivers of living water
You'll be satisfied

When you stumble
When your will is faint
When you can't rise in faith
I will understand
I never tire
Hope still in me and I will raise you up
On the wings of My Spirit's power
You will soar on high

BACKGROUND

There are no times in our lives when we are beyond God's reach. There are no depths from which He cannot rescue us. Often the biblical images for extreme circumstances refer to the dryness and heat of the desert. Even here God comes to revive with shade and refreshment. When we feel totally incapable of doing anything for ourselves He never fails to meet our needs. "He will not grow tired or weary and his understanding no-one can fathom". (Isaiah chapter 40 verse 28).

MAY

In God's House

PSALM 84

JESUS, MY HIGH PRIEST

THE FEAST

PSALM 23

PSALM 84

How lovely is Your dwelling-place Oh Lord
Even the birds find shelter within Your house
And I with them would take My place
Approaching near Your altar
If I could only stay and keep
The entrance to Your doors
I would be happier just to spend one day with You
Than to be absent from Your courts

How blessed are they, the pilgrims pressing on their way
To whom You give Your power
Even the valley of weeping
Shall be turned
Into the place of showers
Oh Lord, You are a sun and shield
You give us grace and glory
You will withhold no good thing from Your own
You are the King of Kings to me

BACKGROUND

The house of the Lord is such a sanctuary that the smallest bird, or most insignificant person, can find safety inside it. The psalmist loved the place where God dwelled and would rather have been there as a doorkeeper than to be obliged to be absent for any reason. Part of the psalm depicts the journey which worshippers had to make to the sanctuary. They were encouraged to keep pressing on. God would turn even the low points or valleys of their pilgrimage into places of blessing. The Lord's generous heart is revealed as the writer declares that He will not withhold any good things from the upright.

JESUS, MY HIGH PRIEST

Jesus, my high priest
Clothed in purple, blue and red
Woven with a golden thread
Reflecting holiness and majesty
Jesus can it be?
You, who died in nakedness
Now robed in such a royal dress
And entering the holy place for me
Now I think I see
Why You had to come as man
So that You might understand
And represent us faithfully to God
Offering Your blood
Not only priest but sacrifice
Once and for all You paid the price
That I might wear
A priestly robe like You
So now anoint me with Your oil
That I might please You as I bring
An offering in righteousness
For this world has never known
A King more worthy, Lord, than You

BACKGROUND

*This song was written while meditating on the beautiful robes which Aaron,
the first high priest, had to wear. At the time Israel had no king but God
and these rich garments were the nearest thing to royal investiture. In the
book of the Hebrews we are shown that the Old Testament priests were
fore-runners of Jesus. His priesthood was to be far superior in that He
would Himself make atonement for believers through His own blood. He
would also create a priesthood of believers all of whom, once cleansed,
could make offerings of praise to God. Let us praise Him for the perfect
work He has done and for the new ministry He has given us.*

THE FEAST

Come now, come and feast at My table
Let's enjoy sweet communion
As together we dine
At Calvary I discovered
What loneliness is
That your fellowship might be mine

Fear not, for you know you are welcome
Each guest is invited
To partake of my food
My sacrifice has secured
Peace and forgiveness for you
Eat My body, drink My blood

BACKGROUND

Supremely God's house is like a banqueting hall into which He loves to welcome guests. Particularly during communion services at church but also at other times in our daily lives we can experience the very presence of the Lord. So life becomes a continual feast as we are caught up into the celebration of heaven. Our feasting, however, was purchased at the cost of the suffering of Jesus. Remembering this keeps us dependant on Him and spiritually healthy.

PSALM 23

I love my gentle shepherd
To follow where He leads
To drink His living water
To pasture where He feeds
In this lies my security
My comfort and my rest
I'll trust His tender care for me
His ways for me are best
He is love

For even when I go astray
He rescues me from harm
Forgiving all my foolishness
He takes me in His arms
So fearlessly he faces foes
Who would His flock attack
Prepared to sacrifice Himself
That He might keep them back
He is love

So I will sing my song to You
And I will call You good
For You provide such benefits
No other master could
Your kindness and your sympathy
Will follow me always
And in Your presence satisfied
For ever I will stay
You are love

BACKGROUND

This psalm is so well-known that we can overlook the sublime teaching in it. Sheep are useless if left to themselves. It takes a wise and vigilant shepherd to keep them fit, healthy and on the right path. Instinctively David knew that God would care for him as he had cared for the family flock. David knew from first-hand experience that this was no easy task and at times would prove life-threatening. Yet he trusted in the sacrificial love of his Lord and the constancy of His presence.

JUNE

LOVER OF MY SOUL

A TIME TO EMBRACE

BETROTHAL

THE WEDDING GARMENT

FIRST LOVE

A TIME TO EMBRACE

Oh My love, come now and speak with Me
Respond with joy to My words of grace
For your voice is sweet to Me
And lovely is your face, My dove
And lovely is your face

Come aside under My shadow now
Rest securely in My embrace
May the fruit from My sheltering tree
Be sweet unto your taste

See the winter is over now
And flowers are blooming upon the earth
The fig-tree forms its early fruit
And bird-song fills the air, My love
And bird-song fills the air

BACKGROUND

The references in this song are from Song of Solomon where there is a prolonged dialogue between the lover and the beloved. Here God, the lover, extends an invitation to the beloved to commune with him. The Lord wants intimate fellowship with us. He loves us to come into His presence so that He can see and hear us. During these special times He wants us to be embraced, fed and rested. He has called us out of the darkness of winter into the summer of hope. All around us are signs of joy and fruitfulness.

BETROTHAL

Oh Jesus I love You
You have captured my heart
With Your cords of compassion
You have drawn me apart
Oh glorious Bridegroom
In faithfulness
You have betrothed me to You, Lord
In Your goodness and truth
Have betrothed me for ever
In Your goodness and truth
And I love You
Yes, I love You

BACKGROUND

In Hosea chapter 2 the prophet likens God to a faithful bridegroom who has made a binding marriage covenant between Himself and us. Through his faithless wife God was teaching Hosea what fidelity means. It means going on loving the one who is faithless despite tremendous heartache. God promises to be faithful to us even when we hurt Him through our waywardness. He is continually drawing us closer to Himself through His great love. Our response to this kind of love can only be - I love you - in return.

THE WEDDING GARMENT

Take this robe of righteousness
I have made for you
Wear it like a wedding dress
Fashioned just for you
I designed it in eternity
Carefully chose it
Patiently wove it
The most lovely garment in the world
It was paid for out of sacrifice
Bought without money
Purchased with life-blood
The most costly garment in the world
Wear it with your crown, My queen
And with flowers in your hand
So My beauty and My fragrance
Will be revealed throughout the land

BACKGROUND

In this song I imagine God Himself preparing robes of righteousness for His bride. At the time it was written preparations were being made for a royal wedding and newspapers were full of speculation as to the design of the bridal gown. All that was known was that it would be made from real silk at tremendous cost. Jesus purchased our garment from his own blood. As we wear it we reveal His dazzling beauty to the world.

FIRST LOVE

Bring me back, Lord
To my first love
What I've lost
I long to find
Oh Lord Jesus,
Please re-kindle
All the fervour of Your bride
Like the ring upon Your hand
Place me, Lord, over Your heart
Give me a love
That's as strong as death
A passion that burns
And can never be quenched
Exclusively Yours and of priceless worth
Intimate love that could never be earned

BACKGROUND

At whatever stage we are in our walk with the Lord He will always rebuke us gently if we "forsake our first love" (see Revelation chapter 2 verse 4). He is jealous for the primary place in our affections and will brook no rivals. In Song of Solomon the beloved asks her lover to place her like a seal upon his heart. This refers to the practice of wearing a person's ring close to the heart to denote intimacy. The Lord wants to come that close to us hat we can revel in the intimacy of His great love for us.

JULY

WORSHIP

SPIRIT, SHOW ME HOW TO LOVE HIM

I WORSHIP YOU, LORD

PSALM 116

YOU ARE THE FAIREST

SPIRIT, SHOW ME HOW TO LOVE HIM

Spirit, show me how to love Him
How to bless, how to please Him
Son of God, King of Kings
Let me lose my love of earthly things
By revelation clear that He is here

So, gazing at Your glory
I will kneel, I will worship
I will lift my hands and heart
With my body I will pay the price
Oh Lord, be pleased to take this sacrifice

BACKGROUND

*Jesus told the woman at the well that true worshippers would worship
the Father in spirit and in truth. (John chapter 4 verses 23 & 24).
Only through the power of the Holy Spirit can we truly bless and please
the Lord Jesus. The spirit reveals the glory of Jesus to us and enables
our Spirits to become engaged in worship. In Romans chapter 12
verse 1 we are encouraged to present our bodies as living sacrifices to
God. At times the presence of the Holy Spirit may cause us to kneel or
prostrate ourselves before the Lord. Daily we need to offer our bodies
to God to be used in whatever way he chooses to glorify Him.*

I WORSHIP YOU, LORD

I worship You, Lord
With precious ointment
I want its fragrance
To fill the air
As I now break it
Upon Your feet, Lord
And spread its perfume with my hair

I love You, Lord
For Your forgiveness
I recognise You
For who You are
The Lord of glory
Come down to save us
Our rising sun
Our morning star

I would anoint You
Against Your burial
Knowing Your death, Lord,
Is not the end
You suffered through it
To gain our pardon
And rise triumphant
The sinner's Friend

BACKGROUND

It seems that one of the anointings of Jesus took place shortly before His death. Strangely enough the women who took spices and perfume to the tomb after the crucifixion were unable to use them because of the resurrection. Jesus accepted the extravagant worship of the women who anointed Him, rebuking the critics. Today too He receives honour from those who lavish affection on Him.

PSALM 116

Oh how I love the Lord
For He hears my voice
He has taught me to trust in Him
Whenever in distress
When sorrows overwhelm
And pain is all around
His compassion and sympathy
Are always to be found
Be at rest, my soul
For the Lord has kept
My eyes from tears
My feet from snares
My life from the grave
That I may walk before You
That I may never faint
For You show me how precious to You
Are the lives of saints
What can I give back to You
For all Your love and grace?
In Your house I will sacrifice
A cup of joy I'll raise
For I love You Lord, really love You, Lord

BACKGROUND

As he reviews his life the psalmist sings out a love-song to the God who has always answered his prayers. In times of danger or distress there has always been comfort and deliverance from on high. As he remembers he bids his soul to be at rest in the Lord. Seeking a way to thank God he determines to go to his house and make a sacrifice of praise.

FAIREST OF TEN THOUSAND

You are the fairest of ten thousand
A king among the sons of men are You
Your name is high above all others
Poured out like a pleasing, sweet perfume
And with Your gentleness,
Your love so rare
And with Your holiness
Who can compare?
Come now into Your fragrant garden
Enjoy here my praise and adoration
The worship that belongs to You

BACKGROUND

In the Song of Solomon the beloved declares that her lover is infinitely superior to all other men. He is the one who is outstanding among ten thousand others. How true this is of Jesus. There is no-one who can "hold a candle" to Him. He is head and shoulders above the rest. The mere mention of His name is like ointment or perfume "poured forth". He is deserving of the exclusive worship of our hearts.

AUGUST

GOD AS FATHER

PSALM 139

DADDY

EVER-PRESENT LORD

PSALM 103

PSALM 139

Oh Lord You know
The thoughts I think
The words I speak
When I go out
When I come in
And when I sleep
Before my birth
Within the womb
You wove my frame
You saw my form
Whither from Your presence
Shall I flee?
To the highest heaven
Or deepest hell
Even there Your spirit
Follows still
Watching me
Keeping me
All of my days
Were in Your book
Before they dawned
Countless the thoughts
Of love You have
To me each morn
Praises to You
Such knowledge is
Precious to me
And wonderful

BACKGROUND

This psalm takes us back to our roots. It is a boost to our sense of identity and security to be reminded that God knew everything about us even before we were born. Indeed God tells Jeremiah that he knew him before He formed him and set him apart as a prophet before his birth. Imagine the creative God knitting us together in the womb, forming a totally unique individual! No wonder the psalmist gasps in amazement at such an incredible revelation. The only fitting response is praise.

DADDY

Like a child I long to climb
Into Your armchair once again
Knowing that You will receive me
Confident You will believe me
And trusting You to ease my pain
And to explain that You are always near me

Then once again You'll sing Your song
Reminding me that You are strong
You're my Daddy, I'm your daughter
You're my castle and my fortress
And here, within the safety of Your walls
I am warm. Your fire is always burning

And when I ask You for advice
Your words to me are always wise
As I nestle very close to You
I can hear Your very heartbeat too
Oh Lord, I delight to do Your will
I'm ready still for all Your love requires

BACKGROUND

This song was written when I needed somewhere to go to find comfort. It is based on a memory of the warmest, safest place I knew as a child. It was to sit on my father's knee, especially on a Sunday evening listening to hymn-singing on the radio. The coal-fire would be burning and we would share the big hymn-book. There was such security in listening to his deep voice singing out the old songs. The one I have particularly in mind is "Oh God our help in ages past". At the shaky places of our lives it is good to remember the God who was there before the mountains were made. Our father always welcomes us when we go to Him. He wants us to come close enough to hear the heart that pulsates with love for us.

EVER-PRESENT LORD

My child, I long to show you
That before your life began
I knew you and I loved you
I had you in My plan
And when your form in secret
Was knit within the womb
I watched you and I waited
Until your time was due
When the day dawned for your birth
I rejoiced as you came forth
And I held you in my arms with pride
Though a mother may forget
And a father may reject
From that moment
I have never left your side
The times when you were lonely
And when you were confused
The times you were misunderstood
And when your heart was bruised
In my everlasting love
I have always understood
And will finish what I first began
I am near to touch and heal
And My cross - it was the seal
For your name is carved
Forever on My hands

BACKGROUND

The truth that the Lord has been with us throughout our personal history came as a revelation to me a few years ago. It was a comfort to know that there was nothing I had experienced which He had not gone through with me. The relationship we can have with Him is closer than the ones we have with our natural parents. We can bring the bad experiences of our past into His presence so that we can have healing and a sense of peace about them. The proof of His love for us is in the marks on His hands.

PSALM 103

Just like a father
You pity us Lord
With great compassion
Remembering we're dust
For like the flowers
We flourish then fade
Our days are fleeting
How quickly they pass

Oh God of mercy
Abounding in grace
You never treat us
Just as we deserve
Your love transcends
All the evil we've done
Just as the heavens
Are high above the earth

How shall I thank You
For all that You give
Healing, forgiveness
Redemption from sin
You satisfy all my deepest desires
My soul will praise You
From all that's within

BACKGROUND

This song picks out some key themes from the psalm, some wonderful reasons for praising God. The first verse extols His fatherhood. Since He is our father He knows how much we can take. He always treats us with gentleness and compassion. The second verse praises the forgiveness and mercy of God. His steadfast love is so great that it is able to cover our sins. In the third verse we are reminded of the manifold blessings of God. There is no way we can adequately thank Him. All we can give Him is the totality of our soul's worship.

SEPTEMBER

SEASONS

HARVEST SONG

THE GARDEN

COME WITH YOUR PLOUGH

PSALM 1

HARVEST SONG

Praise awaits You, Lord, in Zion
In Your holy habitation
Your chosen priests draw near
To worship You
Where morning dawns and evening fades away
You call forth songs, songs of joy
For You are a God who answers us
By awesome deeds and righteous
Oh God our saviour, hope of all the earth
You made the mountains by Your mighty power
And still the nations with Your breath
How blessed are the people You have chosen
To dwell close to You in Your courts
How blessed are we to be forgiven
And taste of Your goodness Oh Lord
For You crown the year with bounty
At Your harvest full and plenty
Your carts in their abundance overflow
The hills are clothed with gladness as they sing
And Your valleys shout for joy
So we join in celebration
Of the God of all creation
Your streams and showers bless the land You made
Where morning dawns and evening fades away
You call forth songs, songs of praise, songs of joy

BACKGROUND

In psalm 65 David praises the God of creation who crowns the year with His goodness at harvest-time. Everything God creates is given generously and bountifully. Blessing is heaped upon blessing. This psalm makes me think of the little country churches I used to visit at harvest-time when my husband used to preach on the Methodist circuits. They were laden with farm produce. Every available corner of the building was crammed with colourful displays of flowers, fruit and homemade bread. It is little wonder that such a God calls forth songs of joy from one end of the earth to the other.

THE GARDEN

Will you let Me come and take
From your garden spices and fruit
To Me only open the gate
Will you be a true love of Mine?

Will you let My spirit blow
On your garden softly or strong
Letting all its fragrance flow
Will you be a true love of Mine?

Will you keep its key apart
Guard it well and let Me drink
From the secret spring of your heart
Will you be a true love of Mine?

BACKGROUND

*In Song of Solomon chapter 4 there is the image of the beloved's life
as a garden to which her lover enjoys coming. He expects it to be a
place of refreshment and fruitfulness which is kept beautiful for Him.
We can draw a parallel here between the life of the Christian and the
Lord Jesus. He wants us to keep a special place in our hearts for
intimate communion with Him. At times the winds of the Holy Spirit
will seem to blow harshly, bringing difficult circumstances into our
lives. At other times He will act more gently. Through all situations
He seeks to produce growth and the fragrance of Christ in us.
Primarily we belong to Him and He should have first claim on the
fruits of the Holy Spirit in our lives.*

COME WITH YOUR PLOUGH

Come with Your plough
Disturb the ground
Break up the crust of my resistance
And as You drive
Lord, bring to life
The fruitless dust
Of my indifference
And even though these changes
Cause me pain
I know its time to seek You, Lord, again
And plant the seeds of righteousness and truth
In these new furrows
I'll wait for You
To swell the tiny grains
Be patient for the spring and autumn rains
Then reap the yellow harvest of Your peace
And Your unfailing love

BACKGROUND

In the life of a farm the processes of ploughing, sowing and reaping are taking place in their seasons throughout the year. Similarly in our lives God takes us through different seasons. At times we may have to endure the plough cutting through areas of our personality which have previously resisted the Spirit of God. However, as we endure and wait patiently for God to bring times of refreshing, harvest will eventually come. The prophet Hosea cried out, "it is time to seek the Lord". (Hosea chapter 10 v. 12). It may be time for us to ask if God wants to begin some new work in us.

PSALM 1

How blessed is the man
Who refuses to walk
In ways of the godless
But chooses Your law
Your word is His study
By night and by day
His sole meditation
Delight and great joy
Like a tree by the water
With roots that go deep
Giving fruit in its season
Evergreen in its leaf
He will prosper and flourish
All he does will be blessed
Yes, the righteous will know
What is true happiness
The wicked are not so
Like chaff that the wind blows
Unstable, unfruitful
They drift and they die
They will fall in Your judgement
They will fail to be blessed
And the righteous alone
Will find true happiness

BACKGROUND

I originally called this song "Happiness". In the contrast between the Godly and the unrighteous which this psalm draws, the righteous are called "blessed" or happy. They are always stable and productive whilst the ungodly live a life which is fruitless and inconsequential. The secret of the happiness of the Christian is in his love of God and His word. Meditating on the bible is like putting down roots into the very source of life. In whatever circumstances or season of life he finds himself the Christian will consistently produce fruit as He abides in Jesus.

OCTOBER

TRUST

MORE THAN CONQUEROR

PSALM 16

HINDS FEET ON HIGH PLACES

PSALM 121

MORE THAN CONQUERORS

What can separate us from the love of God
Shown to us in Jesus Christ our Lord?
Can trouble, danger or starvation
Persecution, nakedness or sword?
He who did not spare His son but gave Him
Fullness of salvation to provide
Will He not, with Him, give us all things?
Will He not be always on our side?
Who can condemn?
Who will accuse?
God will all charges refuse
Jesus who died
Now lives to defend us
At the Father's right hand
We are more than conquerors through Jesus
I am fully confident that we
Can rest securely in His love for us
Trusting in His cross will always be our victory

BACKGROUND

Whenever I consider the triumphant verses at the end of Romans chapter 8 I picture a court scene. There are times in the life of a Christian when he feels on trial, accused, guilty. At such times we need to think of the Lord Jesus as a skilled defence lawyer who appeals to God on our behalf. The most eloquent plea He has is based on the evidence of His own blood which He gave for us out of His love. The love of the Father Himself is on our side. Was it not He who willingly gave the Son in the first place? Knowing the love of God we have everything going for us. There is no place for condemnation and no circumstance can distance us from that love.

PSALM 16

Keep me safe, Oh God, My refuge
For I am trusting in You
Those who serve other Gods
Find sorrows following
My sacrifice I will bring
Only to You

Apart from You, Lord
I have no good thing
You are my portion and cup
You're my inheritance
Here in your family
The lines have fallen for me
So pleasantly

With my eyes fixed on Your face, Lord,
Never shall I shaken be
I sense You everywhere
Always at my right hand
Whispering counsel to me
So graciously

My heart is glad and my tongue rejoices
Safe from the grave I will be
You could not leave me there
Now that I know Your love
Tasting Your pleasures I'll be
Eternally

BACKGROUND

This psalm speaks of the joy which results from a life of trust in God. By contrast those who give themselves over to any form of idolatry will find it only leads to suffering. David likens God to a full cup of wine or the inheriting of a good piece of territory. Among the saints he finds a loving family. The presence of the Lord is such a reality and delight to Him that he cannot imagine ever being left to himself again. Even in death he believes that he will not be cut off from the pleasure God has given him in life.

HINDS' FEET ON HIGH PLACES

Though there be times of weakness
Failure and disappointment
Though I have faced confusion
When all around seems hopelessness
Yet You are my salvation
You are my strength and song
I will rejoice, I will rejoice in You
To You my love and praise belong
You make my feet like hinds' feet
That I may rise and climb
To share with You
The view from heights above
To draw upon Your grace divine

BACKGROUND

The basis for this song is found in Habbakuk chapter 3 verses 17 - 19. What God had revealed to the prophet was a bleak future in which judgement was to come. Despite the prospect of crop failure and little harvest the prophet determines to find joy and strength in God. He imagines himself to be like a deer which is able to climb the highest mountain. From such a spiritual vantage point he shares God's perspective and becomes secure in the knowledge that God is in complete control.

PSALM 121

I will lift my eyes to You
My creator, helper
Keeper of my soul
When my heart is overwhelmed
I will trust You for refuge
For shelter from the storm
For You are strong
And never sleep
And Your love is
Steadfast, true and deep

I will sing my praise to You
Jesus, Saviour, Redeemer
Lover of my soul
For You listened to my cry
Made my feet firm
My paths straight
You set me on a rock
You are the way, the truth, the life
And I love to
Worship You, my Lord

BACKGROUND

It is good to consider that the Lord never falls asleep on duty. His self-perpetuating energy ensures that He is always awake and watchful. The hills which the Lord made are a reminder that He is the creator of heaven and earth. If He is able to form such majesty out of nothing He is more than capable of bringing help to His created beings. He is utterly trustworthy and protects us from all harm.

NOVEMBER

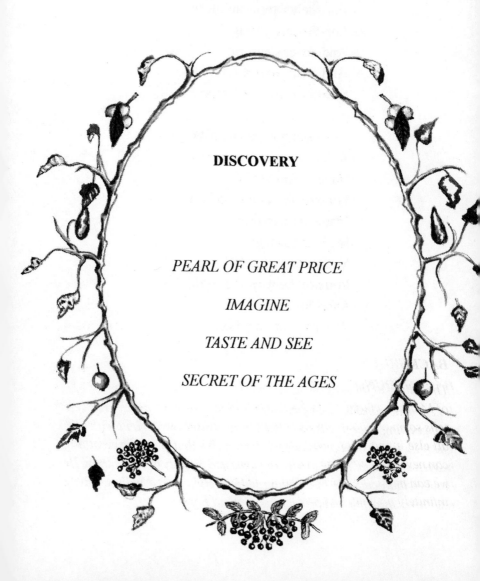

DISCOVERY

PEARL OF GREAT PRICE

IMAGINE

TASTE AND SEE

SECRET OF THE AGES

PEARL OF GREAT PRICE

I love You Jesus
Like the costliest pearl
Your perfect beauty
Satisfies my soul
Yes, You are precious
And Your righteousness fine
Has shone through ages
Before the dawn of time
And like a merchant I have sought
Far and wide throughout the earth
In search of jewels
To bring me wealth and pleasure
Finding You so rich and rare
Has made me give up all I care for
That I might just possess
This single treasure, this pearl of great price
I love You Jesus
Like the costliest pearl
Your perfect beauty
Satisfies my soul

BACKGROUND

The telling of the parable of the pearl of great price is found at the end of Matthew chapter 13. The story takes up only two verses and yet it tells so much about how we should value the Kingdom of heaven above all else in our lives. Jesus is the Kingdom personified and His worth can never be measured. Suffice it to say that He is worth every sacrifice we can make. Discovering Him is to come into possession of the most infinitely precious treasure.

IMAGINE

Imagine that the sun
Failed to give its light
Imagine there to be no moon
Or stars by night
Only if you can imagine
These laws to cease
Would I forget My people
Says God the Almighty
Imagine you could measure
The heavens above
Uncover all the treasures
That earth can give
Only if the tides
Should forget to turn
Would I reject My people
For what they had done
No! I will make
A covenant of peace
To be Your God
And write My laws
Upon Your hearts
The small and great will know Me
The time has come
For men to rediscover My steadfast love
Though mountains may be shaken
And hills removed
Eternally I will have compassion on you

BACKGROUND

The scriptural basis for this song is in Jeremiah chapter 31 verses 33 - 37. Here God reaffirms His love for His people saying it is more unchangeable than the established laws of nature. He also promises to make a new covenant with Israel. In Hebrews we read that Jesus is the mediator of this new covenant. Through Him we receive forgiveness and the Holy Spirit who enables us to know and keep God's law.

TASTE AND SEE

Whatever may befall
His song shall always be
Consistent on my lips
Let men rejoice to see
That those who look to Him
Are never put to shame
Come bless the Lord with me
Let us exalt His name
Oh taste and see
The Lord is good indeed
The hungry He will feed
He satisfies all needs
His tender heart
Is grieved when we are crushed
His Spirit comes to bind up
And when the righteous cry
In trouble or in fear
He listens to their prayer
His angels they are near
My soul shall boast in Him
My refuge and my light
Redeemer of my soul
And keeper of my life

BACKGROUND

Psalm 34 is the basis for this song. The psalm was written at a time when David was on the move to escape the hand of Saul. In such circumstances David was far from secure and yet he resolved to continue to give praise to God. He recalled past deliverances and affirmed his belief in a God who always responds to the cry of distress. Only the man who consistently trusts Him can know His goodness in experience. It is to be tasted and enjoyed rather than just believed in and David invites others to prove God too.

SECRET OF THE AGES

Now the secret of the ages
In a baby of Mary is revealed
Heaven's curtains have been opened
On a mystery long-concealed
Kings and shepherds bow in wonder
I have found You!
I've discovered my destiny
My purpose in You
And I open too my treasures
To offer You the worship that's due
For the seed God gave to Mary
Has been planted in my heart
Christ in me, the hope of glory
Life eternal now can start
And I bow in breathless wonder

BACKGROUND

In Colossians chapter 1 verses 25 - 27 Paul speaks of the "mystery, which is Christ in you, the hope of glory". That Jesus should come and live within people by the Holy Spirit was God's plan throughout the ages. It was only made known to us by the preaching of the gospel through the early apostles. Finding that Christ can live within us by faith is also to discover our individual destiny in life. This discovery leads to a sense of wonder which can only be expressed in costly worship. Our response is to give the best we can offer to the Lord.

DECEMBER

CHRISTMAS THEMES

ZACHARIAH'S SONG

I WILL MAGNIFY

GIVE ME A HEART

THE INDESCRIBABLE GIFT

ZECHARIAH'S SONG

Praise to You, God and King
For our Saviour has come
From David's house He came down
To redeem our nation
Bringing us Salvation
That through faith in His name
And in what He has done
He might bring many sons
Out of condemnation

He can never forget promises He has made
Covenant He has kept
To destroy our enemy
Showing us His mercy
Like the sun He appears
As a light to our path
To dispel all our fears
Breaking through our misery

BACKGROUND

When his voice is restored after the birth of his son, John the Baptist, Zechariah breaks into this prophetic song. It speaks of the coming of Jesus, already conceived in Mary this time. Through the Holy Spirit Zechariah is given insight into the nature of the ministry of Jesus. He is to be Saviour and Redeemer, bringing forgiveness and peace to the earth. Although Jesus is not yet born, Zechariah praises God as he sees His mission already fulfilled and His light breaking through the darkness. In the Spirit time-scale is unimportant. Zechariah had broken into the future.

I WILL MAGNIFY

His greeting troubles me
Oh Lord, what can this mean
That You should choose me
As part of Your plan
I know that through the years
You've answered all my prayers
And now Your promises ring in my ears
"You will be with child
And give birth to a son
To be called
'The Son of God the Most High'"
My spirit sings with joy
And I will magnify
The God and Saviour
Who has honoured me so
The God of history
Now has included me
In a story the future will know
He has filled the hungry
The rich and proud He sent away
He has lifted up the humble and poor
You've been so faithful, Lord
To all You've said before
Blessed are all those
Who trust in Your word

BACKGROUND

This song is based on the visit of the Angel Gabriel to Nazareth and on the Magnificat, Mary's beautiful prophetic song found in Luke chapter 1 verse 46-55. There was a response of joy to the greeting of her cousin Elizabeth who calls her "blessed" among women. It begins as a very personal song but becomes universal and eternal in its perspective as the Spirit takes over and gives her insight into what the coming of the Lord Jesus will mean. Some of the phrases in Mary's song remind us of Hannah's prayer in 1 Samuel chapter 2. In the choosing of His special women at crucial times in history, God truly lifts up the humble and fills the hungry with good things.

CHRISTMAS PRAYER

Give me a heart that magnifies Your name
Like Mary, Lord, rejoicing in my Saviour
Ready for all Your good and perfect will
Treasuring what You gave at Christmas time

Give me a heart that senses when You come
Like Simeon who listened to Your voice
Moved by Your Spirit, waiting for Your hope
Blessed with the vision of Your Holy One

Give me a heart of thankfulness and praise
Like those of old, prepared to follow far
Offering gifts of rare and precious worth
Bowing in wonder as I kneel and gaze.

BACKGROUND

In this prayer the believer asks God for a heart which is similar in attitude to those who worshipped God at the time of the nativity. If we are to follow Mary's example our hearts will be joyful, obedient and full of worship. The example of Simeon encourages us to ask God for hearts that are sensitive to the voice and movement of the Holy Spirit. Such hearts will, like Simeon, be rewarded by seeing what has not been revealed to others. Finally, there is the example of the Magi who patiently sought out the baby King and gave Him their treasures. What other response can we make at Christmas time as we consider what God has given us?

THE INDESCRIBABLE GIFT

So unexpected, so undeserved
The gift that the Father
Sent to the world
How can I thank You
For Your generosity?

Extravagant giver, lavish and kind
Choosing the best
That heaven could find
Such priceless treasure
As Your one and only Son.

As I unwrap it, day after day
Increasing delight flows
What can I say?
So indescribable
The joy that You have brought
To my life.

BACKGROUND

To receive Jesus is to take possession of a gift which can never be adequately described. In Colossians 2 verse 3 we read that in Him "are hidden all the treasures of wisdom and knowledge". Discovering all that is in Him will take more than a life-time. The daily "unwrapping" of all that He contains will continue to give us joy, not just at Christmas but all year round. In 2 Corinthians chapter 9 verse 15 Paul thanks God for His "unspeakable" or "indescribable" gift.